HOW TO SAVE MONEY BY PLANNING YOUR OWN WEDDING

Steps and Tips Making a Cheap Wedding Look Expensive

Melina Cooper

Table of Contents

Five Budget-Friendly Centerpieces
(That Look Expensive)

Though a lot of things have changed in the last few decades, the desire to get married has not. Ceremonies and receptions are still planned, just in a different way. As more and more couples become concerned with their budgets, cost-effective, yet personal weddings have become increasingly popular.

The right centerpiece really adds to the ambiance of the celebration. Beautiful centerpieces do not have to cost you an arm and a leg. Floral arrangements are typically the reason why centerpieces cost so much. By focusing on non-floral and creative materials, you will have a uniquely beautiful and budget-friendly centerpiece. Let's look at five ideas for centerpieces that look rich, but are really inexpensive.

> 1. **Orchid Plants as Centerpieces:** An orchid plant can make for an exquisite, yet simple centerpiece. They can be a great alternative for traditional floral arrangements. Orchids will add some color without taking up too much space on the table. Aside from aesthetics, orchids are also inexpensive. It is not uncommon to find a gorgeous orchid plant for below twenty dollars. If you order in bulk, it may be even less. As a bonus, the plant will continue to live on past the event. They would make lovely gifts for your special guests.

2. **Pillar Candles for Centerpieces:** Pillar candles are classic and elegant. Arrange them into different sizes and then tie with a ribbon to finish the piece. These are the perfect option for those on a budget, as they are reasonably priced and readily available at craft stores. You can help personalize the piece by choosing appropriate colors and scents. Adding ribbons, pine cones or greenery will help to create a striking table decoration.

3. **Paper Flowers for an Elegant Centerpiece:** Do not let the words "paper flowers" scare you! This is not a child's art project. Paper flowers can be very elegant if they are created with the right materials. Die cut paper flowers are a phenomenal way to create a craftier look. If you would like to take a more hands-on approach, consider purchasing a pattern, hand-cutting the flowers and assembling them. You may also choose to purchase pre-assembled pieces. How elegant your centerpiece looks will depend on the paper you choose. If you create your centerpiece out of construction paper, it will certainly look cheap. Instead, look for elegant and unique papers.

4. **Using Wedding Favors as a Centerpiece:** Wedding favors can double as centerpieces when tastefully arranged. By adding a few candles, you can create a charming piece that

allows the couple to show their appreciation to guests for attending. A tip: Place the arrangement on top of a circular or square mirror. Square mirror tiles can be purchased at home improvement stores, while circular ones can typically be found at craft shops.

5. **Using Food as a Centerpiece:** It may seem peculiar, but food is becoming a very popular table decoration. If done properly, the results are quite chic. Arrange fruits and/or vegetables in a cluster to create an exquisite centerpiece. Pears, apples, pineapples and star fruits are perfect for this kind of display. Consider choosing seasonal fruits or vegetables. Nuts are great for fall or winter weddings.

Try to think outside of the box when creating your centerpieces. Not only will they be unique and attractive, but also cost effective. It is great when things *are* not expensive, but they *look* expensive!

Save Money by Planning Your Own Wedding

In recent years, wedding planners have become extremely popular. It really has become the 'norm' to have a planner take care of the details. Once upon a time, the couple and their parents took care of the arrangements with a little help from friends and family. Yes, a wedding planner is helpful, but they are not a necessity. In actuality, you will save yourself a lot of money by taking the wedding planning into your own hands. If you are a couple looking to save money, there are two reasons why you should think about planning your own wedding.

By Planning Your Own Wedding, You Will...

A. **Save Money**: By not hiring a wedding planner, you will, of course, save yourself quite a bit of money. The fees for a planner vary, but are largely dependent upon how involved they are in the planning process and their experience level. Location will sometimes affect the cost as well. If you choose to plan the wedding yourself, you cut these costs out completely.

B. **Avoid Unnecessary Spending**: A planner is likely to present you with a hundred new suggestions for your wedding, all of which will drive the price through the roof. Some planners are quite persistent about adding special elements and while they may have the couple's best interest in mind, things can get out of hand rather quickly. Before you know it, you have gone way beyond your budget. By doing the planning yourself, you will be able to avoid any pricey suggestions, unless, of course, you bring them upon yourself!

Some planners claim they save their clients money by providing them with special deals or referring them to certain vendors. In certain cases, this is true. However, you will still keep overall costs down by doing the job yourself. Here are some tips:

Make Use of Talented Guests: You may want to take advantage of some of your more talented guests. Skilled bakers may be able to help with the wedding cake. A talented singer may be able to provide entertainment. Ask them if they would be interested in helping you out. Just be sure that you are not giving them the impression you only invited them because you wanted to use their skills.

Recruit Your Friends: In all likelihood, your friends will be just as excited about your wedding as you. Most will be glad to help you shop for flowers, find the perfect dress, or search for the ideal reception location. After all, this is what friends do. If you are uncomfortable assigning friends with jobs, be sure to ask your newlywed pals for tips or advice. They can share their experiences and maybe even give you a heads up about certain problems you may run into.

Delegate Jobs: Put your wedding party to work by giving them some jobs. It may be a good idea to consider the personalities of your group when handing out job assignments. Do not put 'Irresponsible Irene' in charge of booking the reception hall. Leave that assignment to someone you can trust. Giving the wrong person the wrong job may cause you more problems than you agreed to.

Learn to Bargain: Wedding planners like to boast that only *they* will be able to offer you one-of-a-kind-deals. The truth is you can find deals on your own. Resolve yourself to never paying full price. Learn to haggle and be persistent. When economic times are tough, vendors will be happy to negotiate, as they are looking for any kind of business. Once you have successfully made a few deals, pat yourself on the back for saving quite a bit of money.

Even if you have no idea where to start, there is really no need to hire a wedding planner. There are plenty of couples that have planned beautiful weddings and did it without the help of a planner. You do not need to break the bank to have the wedding of your dreams.

Fun Alternatives to Traditional Receptions

When most people picture their wedding reception, they imagine guests sitting down for a formal dinner, or buffet, at a rented hall. After enjoying a full meal, everyone "lets loose" and celebrates. Guests enjoy music, cake and alcohol is typically served.

For couples looking to save a little in this area, there are alternatives to the traditional wedding reception. It is the perfect opportunity to do something out of the ordinary. Some fun alternatives include: A picnic reception, barbeque reception, cake and champagne reception and cocktail reception.

A Fun Barbeque Reception: This is perfect for couples looking to have a warmer, more intimate wedding. Barbeques are fun and down-to-earth. The menu can consist of sausages, steak and chicken, along with some side dishes and drinks. Barbeque receptions can be held at the marrying couple's home or even at one of their parents' homes.

A Picnic Reception: For couples getting married in the spring, summer or fall, this is a wonderful choice. Celebrating outdoors and enjoying traditional picnic fare is a fun and unique way to host a reception. Not only will it create a more laid back atmosphere, but because the food served at a picnic is typically

10

inexpensive, you will be able to cut costs. Traditional sit-down dinners and buffets can be quite expensive. The two of you may choose to cook the food ahead of time, or cater it yourselves. If the guest list is on the small side, this should not be too difficult.

A Cake and Champagne Reception: This kind of reception is relatively inexpensive. Rather than serving a full meal, guests will enjoy some cake and champagne. By going this route, the couple can still have a classy reception, but cut down considerably on the traditional costs. Choose a high-end champagne and delectable cake. Focus your spending on these few items to really make your reception shine.

A Cocktail and Snack Reception: A cocktail reception is a great alternative to a traditional reception. Rather than serving a full meal, guests will enjoy drinks and some light snacks. Just be sure to inform guests that a cocktail reception will be held after the ceremony. This way, nobody anticipates a full meal being served.

While planning an alternative reception, try to remember that this is *your* wedding. People may tell you that it is a faux pas or that you just can not do things this way. This is your special day and your loved ones will ultimately be overjoyed to be a part of it. It does not matter if you are knee-deep in mud, or outside of Westminster Abbey.

Budget Wedding Venues

For many couples, the surprise of learning that they must pay for the wedding venue can prove quite overwhelming. Whether you choose an outdoor setting, a church, temple, or hotel, you must pay to rent them out. For couples on a budget, finding a wedding locale that does not charge extravagant rental fees or catering costs is a must. There are quite a few budget options available.

A Banquet Hall: Banquet halls make lovely wedding locales. Most are rather inexpensive, and when decorated beautifully, can be an excellent place to hold a wedding. These halls typically have plenty of space to seat guests and are already equipped for catering and food preparation.

A Park: This is a rather popular venue for couples to hold their wedding. Most are already decorated and are either free or inexpensive to rent out. If you are planning a park wedding, be sure to make arrangements with the park's administrators to make sure that there are no other wedding or events planned for that date.

A Beach: Beaches can make for breathtaking wedding locations. Not surprisingly, this locale is highly sought after. Beach weddings are typically more relaxed and fun. The ocean makes for a beautiful setting. Another plus is that travel expenses are excluded if the couple and their guests already live near a beach.

A Theater: For a unique and dramatic wedding, consider holding your ceremony at a local theater. These venues are typically inexpensive to rent and may come with adequate space for your reception.

A Church: Churches are a very popular choice for a wedding venue and their rental fees are budget-friendly. Some churches offer their venue to church members at no cost. If you are considering a church for your wedding venue, be sure to get in touch with an administrator, specifically the person in charge of weddings. They will provide you with all of the important details.

A Private Residence: Holding a wedding at a private residence is, arguably, the most cost-effective option. The home may belong to the couple, a friend, or their parents. One nice advantage to this locale is that the setting is much more intimate. This is an ideal choice for couples with a smaller guest list.

Couples are happy to learn that many options are available to couples searching for a cost-effective wedding locale. It is absolutely possible to have a wedding that's beautiful, but will not break the bank.

Wedding Planning Tips to Save Money

When a couple gets married, they embark on a new life together. Because of the importance of this event, it was not uncommon, at one time, for the bride's parents or the couple themselves to spend their life savings on the occasion. As the economy shifted, and more individuals found themselves unable to hold a steady job, people subsequently changed their priorities. They no longer have the means, or desire, to spend their savings in such an ardent way. It has become more common for couples to plan their wedding in a more frugal way. Listed below are various ways to cut costs and save some money while planning your wedding.

Shop Off-Season: For the best prices, try to purchase your favors and other wedding items during the fall and winter months. By this time, wedding season will have passed, and most items will be offered at a discount. You may also want to consider getting married during off-season months as you may also be able to snag discounts from vendors as well.

Forget Hiring a Wedding Planner: No matter what you have been told, it is absolutely not necessary to hire a wedding planner. By planning your wedding yourself, you will save a lot of cash and avoid the pressures of tacking on extra expenses for unnecessary details.

Choose Bigger Tables: Bigger tables also mean fewer tables. This, in turn, will mean using less tablecloths and centerpieces. You may also be able to fit more people into a smaller location.

Shop *after* Valentine's Day: Couples purchasing their wedding favors or decorations may want to try shopping around the holidays. Just after Valentine's Day has passed, you can find plenty of wonderful love themed decorations or candies at a bargain price. This is also the perfect time to find the right items for your wedding favors. They are appropriate for the occasion and come at an affordable price.

Take Advantage of Your Venue: Save your guest's time and your time by using one location for your ceremony and reception. This way, you will avoid having to pay double the amount in rental charges. Vendors that charge by the hour will not have to travel from one location to another, thus cutting their fees. Contact your venue and find out if you can receive a special deal for holding both your ceremony and reception at their location.

Be Picky About Your Guest List: A couple may want to invite all of their acquaintances and family members, but keep in mind that each guest comes with a price. If you are looking to hold a traditional wedding, you will need to pay for favors, dinner and drinks. A guest list with a hundred plus people will become very expensive, very quickly. While it may be uncomfortable for the bride and groom, the guest list should be narrowed down to individuals that are closest to the couple and who deserve to have a place at a table.

Choose One Signature Cocktail In Lieu Of a Full Bar: Rather than offering guests a full bar, consider offering one signature drink to serve. In doing so, you will cut down on costs. Another option is to stick with wine and beer and nix the hard liquor.

Choose Flowers That Are In-Season: A big way to cut costs is to choose flowers that are in-season. Out of season flowers are very pricey. For example, if your wedding is in May, Lilies will be readily available and cost-efficient. However, Roses or Amaryllis would cost you a pretty penny.

With just a little creativity and some extra planning, a wedding can be both affordable and elegant.

Skip the Flowers and Save Big

Did you know that flower-free weddings are significantly less expensive? A wedding can be a very costly occasion, so cutting costs wherever possible is important. It may sound ludicrous to skip the flowers, but by doing so, you will save yourself a lot of money.

The average cost of a wedding is $20,000 in the United States. Certain areas of the country have an even higher average. So, how much of that $20,000 is flowers? Try $5,000, and oftentimes it is even higher. There are plenty of flower alternatives to make your wedding ceremony and reception beautiful. Floral-free centerpieces and decor are much less expensive and can be very pretty.

By choosing to hold your reception at a botanical garden, park, or other outdoor venue, your guests will still be able to enjoy beautiful greenery and flowers, without costing the couple a dime.

Add some ambiance to your wedding with candles and some low-key lighting. Both are inexpensive and can influence the feel of the room. Candles can be purchased in bulk for a discounted price at craft stores. Lanterns make for beautiful, contemporary lighting solutions that can be used at the ceremony and/or reception. They can also double as chic centerpieces.

Tiki torches are another fun, inexpensive alternative for those having summer or beach weddings.

For those who still want some greenery, but can live without the flowers, you may want to consider purchasing some large plants. They will add a splash of color and some life to the environment. Larger plants can be used for decorating the reception or ceremony and can even be rented, if the couple wishes not to purchase them. Fewer plants will be needed because they occupy so much space.

Using the right fabrics or other natural materials, such as stones makes it possible to create charming decorations. Top your tables with linens that have rich colors and luxurious fabrics. Combine this with centerpieces made of natural materials, like pine cones, for an "outdoorsy" look. Couples that enjoy the outdoors and nature will find these decorations complement their personalities.

By ditching the flowers, you keep more cash in your wallet. The alternative choices allow the couple to be creative and show off their personalities in an unconventional way.

The Ins and Outs of Wedding DIY

When and When Not To Take Matters into Your Own Hands

Some people have personalities that are well-suited for planning a wedding and can make arrangements just as well as a professional wedding planner. In their spare time, they somehow manage to create gorgeous decorations and centerpieces for their wedding reception. Others would rather do *anything* else. To them, designing invitations, choosing linen colors and participating in food tasting are about as appealing as watching paint dry. While anyone can plan their own wedding, some are just not interested in committing to the process. It might be a good idea to leave arrangements to a more qualified person if you hold the following traits.

You Are Bored By Wedding Planning: Some individuals have been waiting their whole lives to plan their weddings and cannot wait to dive right in. Others would rather just enjoy the party. A person who is completely uninterested in the planning process will likely have a poor attitude and may delay making arrangements. In this case, it would be a good idea to allow someone else to step in and take care of the planning. Otherwise, the results could be disastrous.

You Are Unorganized: If you have trouble with organization, you may want to recruit someone to help with the planning. An event of this magnitude demands superb organization skills. Keep in mind that planning a wedding means keeping track of a lot of different details, like venue bookings or any catering arrangements. An unorganized wedding will likely be a disaster. Leave the planning to a responsible family member or friend. If you cannot find a helper, you may need to hire a professional.

You Are Not Charismatic: Making arrangements for your wedding will require a bit of schmoozing on your part. Some people are naturally great conversationalists, while others are on the shy side. To really get what you need for your wedding, you have to be approachable. If you are not a good people person, you should probably leave the planning up to someone else.

You Are a Follower and Not A Leader: Planning a wedding means taking charge. Understandably, very little will get done if nobody takes initiative, so you must be ready to face conflict, delegate responsibilities and learn to negotiate with vendors. If you have trouble in these areas, it is probably best to let someone else take on the job.

To an outsider, wedding planning seems like an easy task. That is far from the case. To be successful, you must have impeccable organization, excellent people skills, and a lot of knowledge. If you are not motivated or excited by the process, you will likely find the task to be overwhelming. There is no shame in asking for help from friends or family. Chances are someone will be willing and able to take charge of your wedding planning.

The key is to be honest with yourself about your capability. If you are not well-suited for the job, let someone else take it on. In the long run, it is the best decision for everyone. You are going to need someone who can take charge and get things done.

Let's Get Crafty: Using Your Own Artistic Skills to Save Money

It is fun to create your own decorations, favors, gifts and centerpieces. It allows you to be crafty while cutting down on some of your wedding costs. It is important to remember though, that no matter how crafty you are, you are not a "super bride" (or groom). You can not take on everything on your own. Do one thing at a time, and be sure to pick and choose your projects carefully. The last thing you need is to frustrate yourself. Rather than pushing yourself to your limits, try delegating tasks to friends or family members. On the other hand, it may be worth spending a little extra on vendors to save yourself some grief. Here are some ideas for you and your crafty loved ones to take on:

DIY Escort Cards: This is a fairly simple project that a crafty bride, or friend of the bride can take on. This is also an opportunity to put a bit of the couple's personality into the mix. Try to think outside of the box as you have a lot of leeway here to be creative. Some ideas include: Mock ticket stubs, votive candles, starfish or paper flowers.

DIY Thank You Notes: Although thank you notes are sent after the occasion, they still hold an important role in the wedding process. After all, you want to make sure you let your guests know you appreciate their attendance and gifts. A little thank you note created by the bride or groom is more personal and inexpensive. Make sure your message is handwritten. Guests will certainly appreciate the effort.

DIY Table Linens: Unless you are a skilled seamstress, you may want to steer clear of attempting to create your own or your bridesmaids' dresses. However, tablecloths and napkins are a rather simple task that even a beginner can take on. This is a much more affordable option and you can match your decor perfectly.

DIY Bridesmaids and Groomsmen Gifts: Another area to add a little personal touch and cut on costs, is with the bridesmaids and groomsmen gifts. Rather than purchasing a store bought impersonal gift, consider gifting a decorative item, scrapbook or some bubble bath. These are inexpensive choices that will also please your wedding party.

There are hundreds of DIY projects a bride, groom, family member or friend can do to help cut the cost of a wedding. Just remember to choose your projects carefully and try not to take on too much at once. You certainly do not want to take the fun out of your wedding, or bring too much stress upon yourself.

Take on a few projects yourself and leave the rest up to others.

Your Wedding Budget: Where Not to Be Stingy

When economic times are tough, maintaining a tight wedding budget is often necessary for the bride and groom-to-be. It becomes unrealistic, or unwise, to siphon their savings into their wedding. While it is very important to take a frugal approach to the wedding planning process, it might be even more important to ensure that you do not take things too far. There are certain areas where a couple should not be "stingy."

Videography: A couple's wedding video holds a lot of sentimental value. Watching the wedding video with friends, family or one another, will allow the memories of the momentous occasion to live on. Without a videographer, a couple loses this privilege and will regret not capturing the event on film. Chances are, a couple's wedding video will be passed on and enjoyed by future generations.

Wedding Photos: Many couples may think they can skip hiring a wedding photographer, or feel this is an area where they can cut back. Remember, wedding photos are forever. Hiring a bad photographer will likely become a regretful decision. For many couples, choosing the least expensive option is often tempting. Just be sure to look at the photographer's work and not their price. Pictures from the big day will be shared with friends, family members, colleagues and children.

The Bride's Hair: A woman's wedding is the one of the biggest days of her life. It is important for her to look and feel beautiful. Her wedding day will live on through photographs and video. Someday, she will share these memories with her children and grandchildren. A couple may want to consider cutting their costs in other areas of the wedding, so that the bride can get a professional hair stylist. Doing her own hair will likely cause her a lot of stress and she may not be happy with the results. A bad hair day is bad enough on a regular day, but to have it happen to a woman on her wedding day is dreadful.

The Bride's Makeup: For many of the same reasons, a woman should also have her makeup done by a professional. Because photographs are involved, a woman's makeup needs to be a bit more dramatic. The bride may not have the skills, or tools, to accomplish the right look on her own. Makeup artists are relatively inexpensive and will help the bride look her best in person and on film.

Wedding costs can certainly be cut in some areas, but not in others. It is important to stay within budget, but not at the expense of the bride and groom's happiness. By singling out the important areas, a couple can better understand where to cut costs, without making any regretful decisions.

Assessing Wedding Vendors:

Does the Service Live Up to the Price Tag?

The vendors a couple chooses to work with can make or break their wedding day. The right vendor will provide their services in a friendly and professional way. Make the wrong choice, and they may find themselves dealing with a rude, flaky and unprofessional organization. The happy couple should do everything they can to avoid the latter. Of course, it can be difficult to ascertain which vendor is the right choice. Here are some tips:

Do Your Homework: While searching for potential vendors, it is important to research each candidate. If possible, ask recently wedded friends or family members for recommendations. With today's technology, it is easier than ever to find information about professional organizations. Look over the vendor's website and check for reviews. Their site will reveal information about what services the vendor provides, appropriate licenses and any associations they may hold.

Do not rush this process! Really take the time to research the company's web presence. Along the way, you may come up with questions to ask during a consultation. Some vendors may also be weeded out at this stage.

Doing a quick search of the organization's name in a search engine, i.e. Google or Bing, will provide you with even more information. There will likely be independent reviews given by past customers. If the results are more negative than positive, take them off the list. Should there be little or no information on the vendor, it may be best to avoid them as well. No presence is sometimes worse than a poor one.

Arrange A Formal Consultation: After weeding through potential vendors, begin scheduling formal consultations with those that are under consideration. Vendors will use this opportunity to share what services they can provide. This is also the time to ask questions or address any possible concerns.

Request References: A vendor's reputation is largely determined by their delivery of the services they have promised. A quality vendor will be able to supply a couple with a nice list of references. Be sure to make use of that list and give each person a call.

Review the Vendor's Portfolio: Always view a vendor's portfolio before hiring them. It can be hard to judge the quality of their work without seeing it first hand. Pictures and samples should satisfy curiosity and allow the couple to weigh each vendor's work. Every vendor will have a portfolio – even florists, musicians, caterers and cake decorators.

Request a Bid: Before a final decision can be made, the couple must receive a bid from a vendor.

Compare Vendors: Once a couple has done their research and participated in a few formal consultations, they can begin comparing vendors. At this point, they will have enough information to make an informed decision. It is important that the couple understand what is included in each quote and that they are comparing the proper vendors. Weighing a caterer against a photographer makes little sense.

Hiring a reliable and trustworthy vendor is critical to the success of a wedding. Part of the process is evaluating potential vendors and is, arguably, one of the important aspects. To thoroughly asses a vendor's capability, the couple must do the appropriate research, contact references, evaluate portfolios, request a bid and compare final vendor choices. At this point, the couple can make an informed and smart decision.

The Ten Best Ways to Cut Costs On Your Wedding

Looking for even more ways to minimize costs, without sacrificing the integrity of your big day? Here are some ideas:

1. Plan the wedding for a Friday or Sunday evening. Saturdays are the most popular for weddings, so it will likely cost more to book on that day. Choosing an off-peak day may also help to ensure that the couple's choice vendors will be available.

2. Forget custom bridesmaid dresses. Gather your bridesmaids together and allow them to pick out a dress off the rack, instead of shelling out the money to have custom dresses made. This will save you hundreds of dollars in fittings and alterations.

3. Go for simple bridesmaid bouquets. Instead of having each bridesmaid carry an elaborate bouquet, consider having them carry one single stemmed flower or rose. The choice is still elegant and classic, but allows the bride's bouquet to really stand out. The bride's bouquet will be

accentuated by the simplicity of the bridesmaid's bouquets.

4. Choose the music wisely. The idea of hiring a live string quartet to play Pachelbel's: "Canon in D" while the bride walks down the aisle sounds beautiful, but it will be more cost effective to use a CD or a church pianist. The same thing goes for the reception's entertainment. A live band is more costly than a DJ. However, a DJ can customize the music to fit the guests' mood.

5. Go for simple invitations. Yes, fancy calligraphy and embossed invitations are beautiful, but the truth is, the invitations are only going to wind up in the trash can. Keep the invites clean and simple. This way, you can spend your money in areas people will enjoy.

6. Ditch the hors d'oeuvres. Passing around hors d'oeuvres will only fill your guests up and leave them unable to enjoy their dinner. If there will be a delay between the ceremony and reception, think about setting up a small buffet of cheese and crackers for guests to nibble on. If possible, take pictures before the ceremony begins to save time. The less time guests have to wait, the better.

7. Keep the guest list short. This can be a difficult task, but it often has to be done. If you know inviting one person means you have to invite a slew of others, cut them from the list. If inviting cousin Stacy means you have to invite cousins Adam, Mark, Lacey and Rhonda, then do not invite Stacy.

8. Have a morning wedding. It may seem unorthodox, but catered brunches or lunches cost a lot less than dinners.

9. Have a local wedding. An exotic wedding in Bermuda may sound like a dream. But when you sit down and consider all of the extra costs, you quickly find it is more of a hassle than anything else. Hotel fees, passports, airfare and multiple meal charges will skyrocket the cost of your big day. Keep it local and take advantage of your surroundings.

10. Consider Eloping. This idea may leave quite a few family members aggravated (i.e. mom and dad), but dropping $20,000 or more on a wedding may seem like a bit too much for some couples. This is especially true if the couple does not have the money to begin with and must go into debt just to have an extravagant wedding.

Review and Further Information to Help Cut Costs

Weddings are a billion dollar a year industry. As mentioned, the average cost is around $20,000. Needless to say, planning a wedding is not only stressful, but very costly. However, an expensive wedding does not guarantee that the night will be one to remember. A savvy couple can have the wedding of their dreams, without emptying their wallets. The goal is to make sure the wedding does not put a strain on the couple's finances. This way, they may begin investing their hard earned money into their new lives. Here are a few extra tips on how you can cut the cost of your wedding, without sacrificing quality.

General

> **Create a Budget**: The best way to ensure that wedding spending does not get out of hand is to set a budget. Figure out how much you can realistically spend, and stick with it. Themed extras can be tempting, but do your best to refrain from going over your limit. A few dollars may not seem like a lot, but over time it begins to add up.

> **Prioritize Your Spending**: Certain aspects of the wedding will be more important to the bride or

groom. Focus the spending on these areas and cut back on areas that are not as important. If the groom is adamant about a particular detail, allow him to have it.

Simplicity is Key: Perhaps the best way to save money while planning your wedding is to keep things simple. You know how the saying goes, "Less is more." It truly is. Do you really need a five-course meal, or over the top decor?

Allow Yourself Time to Plan: Taking the wedding planning process slow is a smart idea. If you give yourself plenty of time, you avoid feeling rushed or stressed by last minute details. If you put yourself in a bind, you may have to wind up hiring a professional to help tie up all the loose ends. This will, no doubt, cost you extra money you may not have had. Having ample time will allow you to shop for deals, rather than settling for what's available. Also, if you choose to use a credit card with miles, you can use this opportunity to build up airline miles that may be used for your honeymoon.

Attire

Consider Consignment Shops: As long as you do not have your heart set on a new dress, you can find great deals at local consignment shops, eBay or even in the classifieds. In almost every case, the dress will have only been worn once. Another option would be to ask a family member if they have a dress. This can add some sentiment to the occasion and save you a lot of money.

Rent a Dress: If you are not overly concerned with being able to save your dress, you may consider renting one. This is certainly a cost effective alternative.

Flirt with Evening Gowns: While a bit out of the ordinary, an evening gown can most definitely double as a wedding dress. Department stores offer gowns that are elegant and relatively inexpensive (and in the right color). The uniqueness of your choice will help make the night memorable.

Look for Sample Sales: Most bridal shops hold annual sales to help get rid of any remaining stock in what is called a "sample sale". Call around, and find out if and when each shop holds their sale. While it takes a little extra planning, you may be able to score a great deal on a designer gown.

Have the Groomsmen Wear Suits: A couple can save quite a bit on rentals by allowing the groomsmen to wear suites in lieu of tuxes. This is a great money saving option for those who are not fussy about matching. Most men in the party will already have an appropriate suit in their closet. If not, it will be a worthwhile investment for future occasions.

Hunt for Group Discounts: If you do decide to rent tuxes, try to hunt down rental shops that will offer group discounts. Some companies will give the groom a free tux if the rest of the party rents their tuxes from that establishment.

Let Bridesmaids Choose Their Gowns:
Bridesmaids often complain about the dresses they are forced to wear. The worst part is that they are stuck with an expensive dress they never again plan on wearing. Allow them to pick out their own dresses and they will feel more comfortable. To keep things coordinated, specify a certain color, or supply a matching shawl for the girls to wear.

Purchase Discounted Shoes: The bride's shoes may seem like an important detail, but in reality, no one is going to see her shoes. Unless the bride opts for a short gown, it is perfectly acceptable to shop for shoes at a discount store. In fact, many can dye the shoe to match their wedding colors, for a nominal fee. Another option is to wear slippers. Not only will you feel comfortable, but you will save yourself a lot of money.

Borrow Items from Friends and Family Members: Friends and loved ones will surely be happy to loan you a few items for your big day. This will add a little sentiment to the event and help guests feel like they are a part of the big day. The bride-to-be can borrow jewelry or the groom-to-be can borrow cufflinks. This can be your "something borrowed".

Create Your Own Wedding Accessories: Some of the most costly details of a wedding are the accessories. Cut back on costs by creating some accessories on your own. Rather than investing in a pricey veil, consider creating your own. The pillows that your ring bearers will carry can also be made by yourself, a trusted friend, or loved one.

Floral Arrangements

Grow Your Flowers: If you are able to plan ahead, it is possible to grow the flowers you would like to use at your wedding. For those who do not have a yard of their own, try asking friends or loved ones if you can use theirs. They are not likely to object to free landscaping. In doing so, you will save yourself a lot of money.

Purchase Wholesale Flowers: If planting your own flowers is not an option, you can search for flower markets that offer wholesale deals. The discount may not be as steep as a reseller would get, but it would certainly be cheaper than purchasing the flowers at a retail shop. Also, by purchasing the flowers in bulk, you will save more. So, consider purchasing all of your flowers from one vendor.

Make Your Own Flower Arrangements: While flower arranging is a bit of an art, it is not as complicated as you may think. Read a few books on the topic, or search the internet for tutorials. If you would like to take it a step further, you may enroll in a flower arranging class.

Reuse Ceremony Flowers: Another money saving option is to reuse flowers from your ceremony for your reception. A florist may be able to transport them for you, or you can enlist a friend to take on the task. There is a risk they will be damaged in transport, but you will save quite a bit by not having to buy flowers for both venues.

Wedding Ceremony

Stick with a Smaller Wedding Party: A smaller wedding party means fewer dresses, tuxes, food and flowers to purchase. This may be able to save you a lot of money. If you are afraid of hurt feelings, consider opting for a best man and maid of honor only.

Pick an Off-Season Month: Wedding season runs from May to September. By choosing a late fall or winter wedding, you can strike some great deals with vendors. It will also increase the chances that the desired venues will be available for booking.

Ditch the Limo: If your dream wedding does not necessarily include a limo ride or some other extravagant mode of transportation, you may want to consider a less expensive alternative. Perhaps a loved one has a unique or vintage car you can use, or you can always decorate your own.

Hold Your Wedding During the Week: The vast majority of weddings are held on weekends, specifically on Saturdays. It is possible to save quite a bit of money by booking the wedding for midweek. If guests and wedding party members are able to make the time work, it can really be cost effective.

Choose an Imaginative Location: For a fun and unique wedding, choose an unorthodox location. A beautiful park or the backyard of a relative or friend can serve as wonderful settings for wedding ceremonies and/or receptions. These venues are far less expensive (some free!) and allow for a more intimate, personal wedding.

Decor

Split the Costs: It may be a smart idea to call your wedding venue and see if any other weddings are going to be held on the same date. If so, see if you can get in touch with the other couple to discuss possibly sharing decor. By splitting the cost, both couples will save money on decorations that will likely not be used after the big day is over.

Be Creative: Allow your wedding's decor to reflect your personality. Choose potted plants, or other natural materials for decorations. Candles, fruit, or other greenery can make for beautiful decorations, but will not break the bank.

Create Your Own Wedding Favors: Wedding favors can be quite expensive, but are relatively easy to make yourself. Customize them to your theme and add a little personal touch your guests will appreciate. If you do not have the time for this DIY project, try recruiting some friends or family members to create them.

Decorate Your Own Tables: Table decorations do not have to be expensive. It is important to think outside the box. Photos of the bride and groom can make for nice, contemporary centerpieces. A simple arrangement of candles can also create an elegant feel, while adding some ambiance to your tables. Be creative!

Wedding Photographs

Do not Settle: As with any other vendor, it is probably not the best idea to just settle on the first photographer with which you meet. A photographer's rate can vary considerably, so be sure to look around for the best deal. Never skimp on quality!

Use a Talented Friend or Loved One: There is a good chance one of your friends or family members is a skilled photographer. With today's technology, it is becoming much easier and economical to pick up the hobby. If you know someone who takes photos that are up to par, ask them if they would take the photos for your wedding. Another option would be to have guests take photos for you. Set up a little competition to see who can take the best photograph.

Look For a Photography Student: For those who cannot afford to hire a professional photographer, consider hiring a student. Just because they are not established yet, does not mean they are not talented. You can post an advertisement in a local newspaper, or on a local university website. Just be sure to view their portfolio beforehand.

Purchase the Negatives: Many photographers will sell couples the negatives from their wedding photos. This allows them to create as many prints as they would like, but at a much lower cost than the photographer would charge.

Use the Photographer for Important Moments Only: It is possible for a couple to cut back on the cost of their wedding photos by opting to only hire them for the important moments. This may mean only hiring them to take ceremony photos. Friends and family members can take photos while the bride and groom are getting ready and also during the reception.

Invites

Create Your Own Invitations: With today's technology, it is perfectly feasible to create your own invitations. Modern printers are capable of working with card stock and can create professional results, at half the price. This option also allows the couple to personalize every little detail.

RSVP by Phone or Internet: Save on postage and RSVP cards by asking guests to reply via the internet or phone. Just include the web address or phone number on your wedding invitation. Make sure your guests understand to RSVP in this manner.

Use a Postcard for Replies: Postcards have no need for envelopes and are much lighter than traditional RSVP cards. This will save you on postage and envelopes.

Entertainment

Create Your Own Ceremony Mix: Rather than hiring an expensive band to play while the bride walks down the aisle, consider making your own CD of your favorite songs. Copies of the CD can be given to guests as wedding favors. If you would like to keep things traditional, you may also bring a CD with a preferred arrangement.

Use a Student Band: If hiring a professional wedding band is not within your budget, you may try getting in touch with a student band, or non-professional. Some musicians may be just as talented as a professional band, although you may lose out on the chicken dance.

DJ Your Own Wedding: It has become very easy for individuals to DJ their own weddings. The bride and groom can create their own mix CDs, or use their iPods, and rent out quality speakers for the occasion. It may be a simplistic approach, but it does ensure that the music played is what guests want to hear and more importantly, what the bride and groom want to hear.

Fare

Ask Friends and/or Family to Cater: If professional catering does not fit into your budget, you may try asking friends or family members to help you prepare the food for the wedding. Guests will enjoy a home cooked meal just as much as a meal that is catered. Remember, this option is much less stressful if the guest list is small.

Cooking for one-hundred or more people may be a bit out of your league.

Choose a Buffet: Buffets may be cheaper alternatives to traditional sit down meals. Less staff will be needed as no waiters are required. Plus, picky guests will have a wider variety of foods with which to choose. This also ensures that guests do not have to wait for servers to bring them their meals. Be sure to ask your caterer if this is a cost-effective option.

Restrict the Open Bar: Couples may choose to limit the open bar to only a few liquor choices, or to be open for only a few hours. If local laws and the venue permits, you may consider purchasing your own liquor and hiring a barkeep.

Purchase a Small Cake: It is amazing what can be done with cakes nowadays. They come in all shapes, sizes and designs. However, the fancier the cake is, the more expensive it is. A sheet cake is a budget friendly alternative that does not sacrifice taste. If photos are a concern, the couple can have a small tier cake for themselves and a larger sheet cake for the guests.

Purchase Food in Bulk: A wedding is the perfect opportunity to take advantage of discount member clubs. Food items and drinks are much cheaper when they are bought in large quantities. Use local discount clubs to purchase some essentials for the wedding. Also, wine and champagne are a lot cheaper when bought by the case.

Choose Unique Desserts: Cake is not for everyone. Other desserts can be much cheaper, but still offer guests that sweet treat they are looking for. Brownies, cookies, pies, tarts, chocolate covered fruits and mousse are all crowd pleasing choices.

Hold a Potluck Dinner: For a more intimate and very cost-effective dinner, ask guests to bring their own dishes to the reception. Have some fun with it and make it a competition. See who cooked the best dish and offer prizes to the winner!

Hold Your Reception During Lunch Hours: Choosing to have an afternoon reception will save on food and alcohol costs. Lunch fare is typically less expensive and your guests will likely limit their drinking.

Choose an All-in-One Venue: Another great way to save some extra money is to hold your reception at a venue which includes everything in their total cost. This way, you can avoid having to rent tables and chairs, or pay for a separate caterer.

Minimize the Wait Staff: If possible, limit the size of the hired wait staff for your wedding. It is important to make sure that you have enough servers, but not so many that some are left with nothing to do. Another option is to hire local college students to do the serving, instead of hiring through the catering service.

Conclusion

Planning a wedding should be a fun and exciting experience. The occasion is a call for celebration and not financial strain. It is possible to have the wedding you have always dreamed of, without going bankrupt. It may not be champagne and caviar, but it will certainly be a night to remember. After all, it is not about the amount of money you spend, it is about the experience you create. All of that extra money you save can be put towards your honeymoon, or purchasing a new home.